A Collection of Poems

Danny P. Barbare

ISBN: 978-81-962026-7-5

First Edition: 2023
Rs. 200/-

Cyberwit.net
HIG 45 Kaushambi Kunj, Kalindipuram
Allahabad - 211011 (U.P.) India
http://www.cyberwit.net
Tel: +(91) 9415091004
E-mail: info@cyberwit.net

Printed at Vcore LLP.

Contents

The Gift 7
A Day in the Sun 8
Hendersonville, NC 9
The Boat 10
Poem 11
The Janitor Preacher 12
The Rainbow's Poem 13
The Red Tail 14
Supper 15
Cold Grapes 16
The Night's Poem 17
Life's Menu 18
Talking About Her Flower Garden 19
Mountain Ride Poem 20
Dad's Silhouette 21
The Apple Orchard and Store 22
The Squirrel's Poem 23
An Acorn 24
The Battle of Autumn 25
God's Poem 26
Portrait of a Broom 27
I Am America! 28
America Says the Janitor 29
Clean! 30
The Independent Janitor 31
A Beautiful Day! 32
A Happy Poem 33
The Janitor's Cloth 34
The Janitor's Muse 35

The Janitor Dusts 36
Dr. Broom 37
The Joke 38
The Carolina Wren 39
Listen to All, Says the Janitor 40
Dusting the Window Sill 41
Cleaning the Showers 42
Working Together 44
Custodial Chores 45
The Janitor Learns to Dance 46
The Broom's Poem 47
The Janitor and His Wife 48
How I See 49
The Accepted Thread 50
Dripping Salsa on the Menu 51
The Hard Worker 52
As If to Shine 53
Us Janitors 54
The Mourning Dove 55
The Janitor 56
Saddler's Creek 57
Friends 58
The Janitor at the Clinic 59
The Work of Art 60
The Janitor 61
The Factory Worker 62
The Janitor at the Medical Clinic 63
To Set the Pen Aside 64
Autumn's Poem 65
Shedding Light 66
The Broom 67
Crossing the Bridge 68
Round and Round 69

The Janitor Speaks America 70
Kid in the Bamboo Patch 71
The Old House 72
A Rich Janitor 73
The Janitor Teacher 74
The Broom Says 75
The Star 76
A Good Dream! 77
Welcoming Spring! 78

The Gift

She'll wrap you
with
kindness
in an assortment
of ways
square as a box
she'll teach.
She's a bread and
butter cookie
mellow and sweet
she'll make you
smile
a gift a treat.

A Day in the Sun

I
get
in
my
penny
of
the
sun

from
dusk
till
dawn

a
mountain
ride
of
copper.

Hendersonville, NC

In the office, in the
box of pictures
this is a photograph
of my Aunt Sally
always wearing
rounded glasses and
having a bible in her
lap as she sat in a
rocking chair on the
porch of her wooden
house, this is my
solid memory, my
poem of her, as if
I can still hear the
gravel road rustling
beneath my shoes.

The Boat

The boat wanted to be a poem
so I let it slip into the
water
and the words began
to float
I turned on the motor
and that gave it motion
like a propeller
the boat had rhythm
across the glassy water
it was evening time as the
lights of it glowed.
It was a peaceful literature
as the wind and water
flowed through my writing
hand.
The ending was a graceful and
quiet wake.
And a sunset across the page.

Poem

Cleaning the windows, I watch
  the jet planes climb into
  the night sky
though my feet are on the ground
  my imagination
  has wings
I fly, polish the glass as high as
  I can reach.

The Janitor Preacher

Pacing myself, it is quite
  the routine
dancing with the barrel
and singing all the way
  bucket to bucket
  as if a dream
of living with the finer
  things
but life can be
  upside down
  and right side up
I have to say: joyfully,
wonderfully, and happily
  empty.

The Rainbow's Poem

Wherever there are clouds,
you are not alone.
Sometimes, rain
drips down the window,
when suddenly the sun shines
a silver lining in the sky,
and you wipe your eyes dry,
as if a rainbow is before you,
like a blessing from up high.

The Red Tail

The
hawk

with
studious
eye

enjoys
his
catch

beneath
the
maple
tree.

Supper

The sausage and sauerkraut
wanted to be a poem.
So I made it sizzle
   word for word
I could smell the sentences
   in the air
taste them upon my tongue.
I swallowed the metaphor
   and simile
till my belly was nearly a
skillet full
of experimental free verse
   served with a ladle
that satisfied me like a song.

Cold Grapes

Cold
grapes

make
me
stop
and
think

how
sweet
they'll
be

when
washed
and
clean.

The Night's Poem

A poem is the light we create in
the night, like the
moon is the
words with a halo
and stars that twinkle
like a diamond—
across the page of a
planetarium like the
little dipper and the
big dipper we scoop
up the ideas, that
shoot across the roof
like the
imagination.
Or the solar system of
planets that are just good friends.

Life's Menu

What is on the menu but who we
are, what we eat. The fertile
soil the farmers till, the
vegetables
the roots of our health.
We are
the sun and rain of the God
that blesses the crops
the water on a thirsty land.
The plate that serves them
the cook at the restaurant.
Or the quaint little garden
we plant the springs forth
with life in summer months
from the precious little seeds
only the Heavens
can make, a dream like
tomatoes juicy and ripe.
The corn
and squash and
other riches of the earth the
love of
nature can provide with
a green thumb and hosepipe.
We are the harvest, the blood of us.

Talking About Her Flower Garden

Words
between us grew
like flowers
in good soil
from roots and
stems
like seeds they
began
pulling out the
weeds
and spreading
pine needles
and water.

Mountain Ride Poem

The mountain ride wanted to be a poem.
The Rhododendron was immortality.
As the flowers were such eloquent
  language.
So I took a pen with bluish-green
  ink
  and wrote across the ridges.
Oh how the words shone with such
  imagery.
As my tongue beat against the roof
  of my mouth
  like the road beat inside me.
The clouds flowed like the French
  Broad River.
Spring was the aroma and sweet
  taste of peaches and strawberries at
  the roadside stand on the way home.

Dad’s Silhouette

I reached out and touched
my father’s silhouette.
I jolted
as if I could go no further.
I awoke in the dark den
laying in the lounge chair.
Turned on the lamp and the
room was silent.

The Apple Orchard and Store

It's autumn. At the end of the gravel
  road
there is a building where they
sell apple butter, cider, chow
  chow
and pepper jelly and other goods.
Some choose to pick their own
  apples
in the orchard
while others by them by the
  bushel or peck full
to last them throughout winter
warm pie for Thanksgiving or
just a golden delicious for a snack
as the snow settles in always a crisp
  bite of fall.

The Squirrel's Poem

The squirrel wanted to be
  a poem
so I told it to hop from word
  to word
and pause for awhile to
  think
then get down to the nut of
  it
or plant the seed in the
  earth
to grow into a tree one day.

An Acorn

A squirrel knawing on acorns by day
dreaming of the orange moon
on crisp nights
getting prepared for the bitter cold
those pointed sharp tips of the wind
autumn's glass
a thin shell of sleep
that might sprout into an oak
sitting on the horizon of a squirrel's' mind
an acorn bouncing down the sidewalk
wearing a wooden hat
and a leaf and stem over its shoulder.

The Battle of Autumn

The leaves have begun
  falling
soon I'll be raking.
Pushing a squeaky wheel
  barrow.
The tarpaulin being drug
  across the grass.
The piles and piles of wind.
The dried bloody colors
  of the sun.

God's Poem

The rain wanted me to write
a poem about it
so I took a pen with colorless
ink
and wrote bubbles across the
sky
like clouds across the paper
till that final click
as the earth was still fresh and
damp till dry.

Portrait of a Broom

Says the janitor
it's a good strong broom
when we have faith in
each other
as that is how the handle
works
straw for straw
we all have worth
especially when quite
kindly sewn together
as if with a red thread of
  blood.

I Am America!

I am the Statue of Liberty.
I am the plump and juicy Blackberries.
I am the Grand Canyon.
I am the Black snake coiled in a tree.
I am the rainbow houses in Charleston.
I am the Loblolly trees.
I am the Aspens and Redwood forest.
I am the lake lapping at the shore.
I am the Blue Ridge Mountains.
I am the pond in the woods.
I am the Key West with its tall bridges.
I am the Gazebo in the park.
I am the Chicago Towers.
I am the boats clapping on the water.
I am the surfers in California.
I am the Cicadas blazing on the back roads.
I am the winter blizzards in the Northwest.

America Says the Janitor

I am the janitor of America.
I have plenty to say.
  Kindness is a yellow
  bucket of water
  and a mop.
It is a good broom.
It is mannerism, etiquette
  and spirit
across the states like shiny
  tiles
like hard work and challenges
  the simple of it.

Clean!

Think
positive

says
the
janitor

as
it
begins
as
a
thread

spreads
light
across
the
desks

like
a
wet
cloth.

The Independent Janitor

Always ready and
willing
as if to never collect
dust.
Oh! How I shine, as
if
my reflection is my
boss.

A Beautiful Day!

Happiness is a blue sky.
A sunny day looking down
on me
that makes me smile and laugh
and even sing
with the
hope and belief tomorrow
will be the same.

A Happy Poem

I want to be happy, so I take
a pen
and write a poem about
the blue sky and sun
and my dream comes true as
if it is set in ink.

The Janitor's Cloth

Says the janitor, happiness to me
is a nice cloth
an index finger
clean as the
windowsill
plain and simple as a smile all around.

The Janitor's Muse

It's creating a poem that
  keeps me working
  like word for
word—broom and mop.

The Janitor Dusts

When the dust settles in
  my mind
I take a rag
and wipe it to a shine
as if without a sneeze
  it is clean
down to the last filament.

Dr. Broom

So the broom
says
sweep away the
ghostly pain
and ache
into the dust pan
and worrisome
bills and
troubles too
straw by straw
in due time
the floor will
shine.

The Joke

A good laugh is a good
  laugh
when the laughter sweeps
  everyone
  across the room
like a humorous talented
  broom.

The Carolina Wren

The Carolina Wren sings on the fence with
its tail
cocked up,
such a tiny bird to
have a sweet, loud song.
It flies away.
Where is
it at? Listen! Chirpy, Chirp! Chirp!

Listen to All, Says the Janitor

I sweep these words
  off my tongue
across the golden grain
where crickets and cicadas sing
I am a janitor
  an American with a cause
who whispers with the wind in
  his voice
softly and proudly with a broom
  listen to all.

Dusting the Window Sill

Have
a
good
afternoon

I
say

it's
a
reflection
on
me

and
I
don't
collect
no
dust
on
the
window
sill
if
there
is
no
reply.

Cleaning the Showers

Scrubbing
the
tile

I
say
to
myself

it
maybe
somewhat
square

but
to
treat
others
with
respect

is
a
shiny
clean
way

to
make
it
in
life.

Working Together

Take criticism and make it
positive says the
janitor
as if it is to be set in ink
like a broom and dust pan
rag and bottle of spray
mop and bucket of water
as that is how we work
together for the
better
and we all shine,
because we all matter.—

Custodial Chores

Wiping
the
black
marks
off
the
wall

as
to
forget
yesterday's
pain

and
remember
the
good
times

like
a
fresh
coat
of
paint.

The Janitor Learns to Dance

Mopping the floor my smile in the shine as if
her little hand is
in the palm of mine
learning to dance
for a Saturday night when the wooden
handle comes to life
no slippery when wet
no caution sign
as if the floor is just drunk on life happily dry.

The Broom's Poem

Always looking
up says the
broom that is how I happily
shine
the wooden handle of it
ain't
know dirt about it
kindness and respect my
bosses linoleum
smile, speaks.

The Janitor and His Wife

Says the janitor
I sweep to hear her
whisper
like a wind across
a golden field.
And I am a willing
ear.
And I mop to
learn how to
dance with her.
And we just have
fun
as if to let it
all wring out
like a bucket of
water.
That is why I work.

How I See

Like a poem I am glass, you can
see
inside me
perhaps see your
own reflection
whether spring summer
fall or winter
I am happy, thanks to
my furnace or
heart this is how I
see,
as if the beautiful magnolia tree.

The Accepted Thread

To accept, says the janitor
a thread
needs to be a part of
a wash cloth
that is how we work together
clean and wrung.

Dripping Salsa on the Menu

Dipping tortillas into salsa is so
addicting
it makes the menu
look less appealing, and
messes up my appetite.

The Hard Worker

My
muscles
may
ache

and
my
bones
grind

but
my
faith
is
strong

and
my
spirit
shines.

As If to Shine

Oh how it shines
says the
janitor
as it is a reflection
upon me—
to my shadow
like a conscience.

Us Janitors

As if to be accepted says
  the janitor
like the broom is to the dustpan
  respectively
or the mop to the bucket
as they work together
  to a shine
  so cleanly with pride
as square and fair as the
  equal tile.

The Mourning Dove

So
peaceful
after
the
evening
storm

somewhere
in
the
church
of
a
tree

a
mourning
dove
does
mourn

or
sing
for
its
mate.

The Janitor

Tonight, I worked with
loneliness. We didn't have
much to say. He followed
me around like my shadow
and complained all day. I
wished I could get rid of him
when suddenly I realized he
was me. And once again I
was happy. Because I had
no one else to blame.

Saddler's Creek

I come
to Saddler's Creek
where the grass
overgrows the road
and blackberries grow
in the red mud ditch
and the wind stirs the
pines and hardwoods.
Crickets chirp and
cicadas shrill, just when
I realize I'm not alone
the water ebbs at my
feet and is blue and
white capping. I have
the lake as wide as
the blue sky.

Friends

Plugged in
the cord fits
the vacuum
cleaner, talks,
listens when
turned off
it has friends
like the
broom and
dustpan, the
dust mop,
and the mop
and bucket
of water too
socially they
have clean
and healthy
friendship.

The Janitor at the Clinic

A
dream

a
bucket
of
water
and
a
mop

so
much
to
wring

there
is
plenty
to
shine.

The Work of Art

It is just another day
to be proud
happy with who I am
with high self
esteem
and the old broom and
mop at hand.

The Janitor

America, from sea to sea I
sweep, hear my words
across this lovely
country
this menial broom of
mine whispers
across the golden fields
and mountains
to bring people to a
smile, to be joyful where
my present being is
I with an attitude of a
grand voice for all to
hear, like the shout
as deep as I can
breathe.
The sun that shines.
My heart to the
multitudes that beats.

The Factory Worker

I am the determined American,
I'm the factory of poems
the cleaner of floors
I hear the hiss, the bang, the clank,
the huff, and puff
the boiler room of words
the creator
I'm the teacher, the educator
steam in the veins
the poet at the podium who speaks
the pistons of power poetically
the maker of poems,
I drink from the bottle of water to
stay cool, the heat
a Nation twenty-four hours a day
the rhythm and rhyme
the peace and calm of ear plugs.
I am the rumble at your feet. The
voice of freedom.

The Janitor at the Medical Clinic

Says the Clorox
with tender majesty
I fight
prevent and prevail
in the killing
fields
my sweet perfume
my rag
my ally
toilet and sink
and wherever it
may hide
wiped asunder
virus, the enemy
with spray, air.
A soldier of clean.

To Set the Pen Aside

Says the good deep blue, I'll help you
write a poem, as if to change your
mood or heart;
as twilight, I'll let you look
inside of me
the beauty of words across the
page
as if eternity is a moment
in time
to look you in the eye
and happily simply be satisfied
to set your pen aside
and as if in awe, you
can say, I wrote this wonderful sky.
A poem I can live with and call mine.

Autumn's Poem

Autumn wants me to write a poem
  about it.
So I take the trees with inks
  of beautiful reds, golds,
  yellows, and oranges
and write in cursive to the
ground with gentle tapping
  of acorns
till the hardwoods are empty
  and the paper
covered, finished with that vibrant
  sound.

Shedding Light

The golden flame touches
the air
or rather the air
touches it
so warmly they
begin
to sway and
dance, like in an oil lamp.

The Broom

I take the good in my wrist
and sweep the floor
clean.
I believe in kindness.
The strength of the wooden
handle broom
I am the janitor of America.

Crossing the Bridge

Heading down to Charleston unrolling
  the hills
I can see the grassy wetlands
along the bridge to the Isle of
  Palms
a White Heron standing on one leg
  cut by the water
a bird without a ripple of clouds
  in its feathers
as there is a cool wind and sunshine
an unrolled window singing the sea.

Round and Round

Time
we'll get it clean
patient as the hour hand
quicker than the red
oh how it happily sweeps
  and hums
shines for the eye
the very face of it
like a smile
broom or rag, the clock or
  floor
round and round we go
like the gears of dawn
  and dusk.

The Janitor Speaks America

I'm the janitor shining these hallways
of promise
of America.
Oh how the linoleum rolling
light
goes from sea to sea
the glory of these students'
dreams
I sweep and dust mop sweet
Liberty
oh how independence sings
so
giftedly like the teachers, students and
me.

Kid in the Bamboo Patch

Into the bamboo patch
a fishing pole to
cut
stung by a yellow
jacket's nest
all night in front
of a fan
sweet sorrow's
rest
till tomorrow at
the pier
deep, blue, cold
oh how nature's
sympathy
tender loving caress
washed of pain and
filled with life's breath.

The Old House

The house was in the woods
dilapidated and broken
with the smell
of age
the shade of the trees
that must have seen
who came and went
through its doors
as the creek still flows
babbles along
the life blood that
remembers
the land
the old as the time is new
no doubt of where it's been.

A Rich Janitor

Things are just things
says the janitor
at the end of
the day
it's how many
smiles
you reflect
oh, how rich you are.

The Janitor Teacher

Cleaning spots on the
wall
with a bottle of spray
and a rag
says the janitor
teacher
it's a good lesson
if you try
like getting down to
the nitty-gritty
rolling up
your sleeves on any job.

The Broom Says

Trust says the
broom you have to
earn it, that's the golden
rule—straw for straw
the very clean of it
that's when my
whisper shines.

The Star

No
matter
how
far
away

Hope
is
a
star

that
finds
her
way
through
space
and
time

and
shines
on
you

and
refuses
to
go
dark.

A Good Dream!

The Bumblebee is buzzing, the Spinner Spider is
weaving its web, the Bradford Pear
Tree is blooming
and the tree with
purple cups.
Spring is not fooling around
down here in the South
winter is just a memory when
you open your eyes
from a nap.
Even the tough little Pansies
are wandering where they are at.
Around here, I know the Azaleas will put it to rest.

Welcoming Spring!

Spring is colors, sweet heavens that
clothe, March you like
fresh wind and rain
a celebration that buttons
you up
stomps in puddles like
rubber boots
like taffy colored
rainbows
and a sunny yellow coat
as flowers pop open like
balloons and trumpet
Bumblebees— be buzzing
busily. This is me my songbird sings.

www.ingramcontent.com/pod-product-compliance
Lightning Source LLC
Chambersburg PA
CBHW022202160726
48282CB00024B/288
* 9 7 8 8 1 9 6 2 0 2 6 7 5 *